Japan Travel guide 2023

2023

Explore Japan: A Comprehensive Guide to its Authentic Culture, Ancient History & Vibrant Cities

Garrett Patton

Table Of Contents

My Experience As a Tourist In Japan

I recently had the opportunity to visit Japan, a country that is nothing short of incredible. I had heard so much about the country and its culture and was eager to explore it. From the moment I stepped off the plane, I was in awe of the beauty and culture that surrounded me. Everywhere I looked, I was in awe of the art, architecture, and the people.

My first stop was Tokyo, a bustling city with a seemingly endless array of attractions. I was instantly taken aback by the sheer size and complexity of the city. Everywhere I looked, I was surrounded by colorful neon lights and towering skyscrapers.

I explored the streets of Shinjuku and Shibuya, marveling at the hustle and bustle of the city. I was also amazed by the breathtaking views of the city from the observation decks of the Tokyo Tower and the Skytree.

I then ventured to Kyoto, a city steeped in history and culture. Everywhere I looked, I was surrounded by ancient temples, shrines, and gardens. I visited the beautiful Kinkakuji Temple and explored the tranquil grounds of the Fushimi Inari Shrine.

I also had the chance to take a leisurely stroll through the beautiful Arashiyama Bamboo Grove, a truly amazing experience.

I then spent a few days exploring the stunning beaches and islands of Okinawa. I was in awe of the breathtaking turquoise waters, white sand beaches, and lush green forests. I took a boat cruise on the emerald waters of the East China Sea and snorkeled in the crystal-clear waters of the Okinawa Churaumi Aquarium.

Overall, my experience in Japan was truly unforgettable. From the hustle and bustle of Tokyo to the breathtakingly beautiful beaches of Okinawa, I was in awe of the beauty, culture, and hospitality of the country. It is a place that I will never forget and that I will always cherish.

Introduction

Welcome to the Japan Travel Guide!

Japan is an incredibly vibrant country with a rich and fascinating history, beautiful sights, and a culture all its own. From the neon-lit streets of Tokyo to the breathtakingly scenic countryside, Japan is a land of endless opportunity for exploration and discovery.

For centuries, Japan has been a place to find solace, to experience the beauty and calm of nature, and to explore the depths of human culture. From the ancient shrines and temples, to the bustling cities and towns, Japan is a land of contrasts and surprises.

Whether you're looking for adventure, relaxation, or a place to explore the culture and traditions of Japan, this guide is here to help. Here you'll find information about the different regions of Japan, the best places to visit, and the best ways to get around. We'll also provide you with tips on how to make the most of your trip, from finding the best restaurants to shopping for souvenirs.

For those interested in history, Japan is a veritable treasure trove of ancient culture, art, and architecture. We'll provide information about the country's ancient history, and the best places to visit for a glimpse of this fascinating past.

And, of course, no trip to Japan would be complete without exploring the country's unique cuisine. From traditional Japanese dishes to modern fusion cuisine, there's something for everyone. We'll provide you with all the information you need to make the most of your culinary adventure.

As the sun rises from the east and lights up the horizon, it is time to explore the land of the rising sun - Japan. With its ancient culture, modern cities, and breathtaking landscapes, a journey to Japan is a treat like no other.

From the bustling streets of Tokyo, to the traditional streets of Kyoto, to the majestic Mount Fuji, Japan is a country of contrasts. Whether you're looking for an urban adventure or a tranquil getaway, Japan has something for everyone.

From the moment you arrive, you will be captivated by the sights and sounds of Japan. The food, the people, and the culture are all unique and will leave you with memories that will last a lifetime.

Explore the ancient temples of Kyoto, or take in the hustle and bustle of Tokyo. Witness the beauty of the cherry blossoms in spring, or explore the snow-capped mountains of the north. With its abundance of attractions and activities, Japan is sure to keep you busy.

So come and explore Japan, a country filled with beauty, culture, and adventure. Wherever your journey takes you, you are sure to discover something new and exciting.

Welcome to Japan.

Chapter 1

Overview of Japan

Japan is an island nation located in the Pacific Ocean off the coast of East Asia. It is a country of stunning natural beauty, with rugged mountains and lush green valleys filled with cherry blossom trees. It is also a country of contrasts, combining ancient traditions and customs with modern technology and the hustle and bustle of large cities.

The geography of Japan is made up of four main islands: Hokkaido, Honshu, Shikoku, and Kyushu. Together, these four islands form the Japanese archipelago, which has over 6,000 islands in total. The capital of Japan is Tokyo, located on the island of Honshu.

Japan has a population of over 126 million people, making it the world's tenth most populous country. The majority of the population is made up of ethnic Japanese, with minorities of Korean, Chinese, and other Asian ethnicities. The official language of Japan is Japanese, but English is widely spoken in cities and tourist areas.

Japan has a long and rich history, dating back to the Jomon period (14,000-300 BC). During this time, Japan was inhabited by hunter-gatherers who lived in small villages and hunted wild animals. By the 8th century AD, Japan had developed into a powerful and unified nation, and the subsequent Heian period (794-1185) saw the rise of the samurai and the development of a feudal system of government.

In the 19th century, Japan underwent a period of rapid modernization, which transformed it into a major world power. In the 20th century, Japan was a key player in both World War I and World War II. Following the war, Japan adopted a pacifist constitution and has since become a major economic power.

Today, Japan is an advanced, industrialized nation with a highly educated and skilled workforce. It is a major exporter of electronics, automobiles, and other goods, and its economy is one of the largest in the world. Japan also has a strong cultural identity, with traditional arts such as kabuki and sumo wrestling, and modern popular culture such as anime and manga.

Japan is a fascinating country to visit and explore. From its stunning natural scenery to its vibrant cities and culture, Japan has something for everyone. Whether you're looking for a relaxing holiday in the countryside or an exciting adventure in the big city, Japan has something to offer.

History of Japan

Japan has a long, rich and fascinating history. From its beginnings as a small agrarian society, to its modern-day status as a global superpower, Japan's history is one of both impressive accomplishment and great tragedy.

The earliest known inhabitants of the Japanese archipelago were the Jomon people, who lived there from around 14,000 BC to 300 BC. They were a hunter-gatherer society, living off the land and worshiping animist deities. During this period, the islands of Japan gradually became more unified, and by the 4th century AD, the Yamato clan had emerged as the dominant power.

Under the Yamato clan, Japan began to develop its first centralized government, known as the Asuka period. Buddhism was also introduced during this time, and it quickly gained popularity as the religion of the ruling class. The Asuka period was followed by the Nara period, which began in 710 and lasted until 794. During this time, the emperor was the absolute ruler of Japan, and a new capital was built at Heijo-kyo.

From the 9th century onwards, Japan underwent a period of civil war known as the Sengoku period. During this time, powerful regional warlords battled for control of the islands, and the country was divided into numerous competing states.

It was not until the 16th century that Japan was finally unified again, under the powerful warlord Oda Nobunaga.

In the 17th century, Japan began to modernize and industrialize, under the leadership of the Tokugawa Shogunate. This period, known as the

Edo period, saw the development of a prosperous trading economy, as well as the spread of culture and art throughout Japan.

It also saw the emergence of the samurai, who served as the ruling class of Japan.

In 1868, the Tokugawa Shogunate was overthrown, and a new imperial system was established. The Meiji period, which began in 1868, saw Japan transformed from a feudal society into a modern industrial nation. During this period, the country underwent dramatic changes in its government, economy, and culture.

The Meiji period ended in 1912, and Japan began to transform itself into a military power. In 1931, Japan invaded Manchuria, and by 1941 it had launched a full-scale invasion of China. In 1941, Japan also attacked the United States, drawing the US into World War II. In 1945,

Japan was defeated by the Allies, and the country was occupied by the US until 1952.

Since then, Japan has undergone a remarkable transformation. It has become one of the world's leading economic powers, and its culture and society have become increasingly modern and globalized.

Today, Japan is a vibrant, prosperous nation, and its history and culture continue to fascinate people around the world.

Culture & Language

When it comes to culture, Japan is a place of contrasts. It is a land of ancient customs, traditions, and rituals—but also of extremely modern technology and industry. With its unique blend of the past and the present, Japan has created a culture all its own.

In Japan, there is a strong emphasis on tradition and respect for the past, which can be seen in many aspects of the country's culture.

One of the most well-known aspects of Japanese culture is its traditional food. Japanese cuisine is known for being healthy and nutritious, with a focus on fresh ingredients. Sushi, tempura, and ramen are just a few of the popular dishes that have been enjoyed by people all over the world.

Respect is one of the cornerstones of Japanese culture. Respect for the elderly, respect for authority, and respect for one another are all deeply ingrained in the Japanese spirit. It is considered rude to speak out of turn, or to interrupt someone. Respect is so important that it is even used as a greeting—the Japanese say "arigatou gozaimasu," which literally means "thank you for your effort."

Japanese people also place a high value on politeness. It is important to be polite and courteous in all interactions, and to be particular about one's language. For instance, to show respect, the Japanese use formal language when speaking to elders or authorities.

The Japanese language is also an important part of the culture. Japanese is an incredibly complex language, with an intricate writing system. It is also very difficult to learn, as it is full of nuances and subtle differences. Despite this, many people have taken the time to learn the language, in order to gain a better understanding of the culture and its people.

The Japanese people are also known for their incredible work ethic. This is especially evident in their highly productive workforce. The Japanese are known for their attention to detail and dedication to their work, which has helped them to become one of the most successful economies in the world.

The emphasis on group cohesion in Japanese society is another significant feature. Japanese people strive to maintain harmony through cooperation and compromise. They believe that working together is the best way to get things done, and this is reflected in the way they interact with each other.

Another important aspect of Japanese culture is its traditional art forms. From calligraphy and painting to pottery and origami, the Japanese have been creating beautiful art for centuries. These art forms are still practiced today, and many people take the time to learn and appreciate them.

The Japanese are also known for their love of nature. Many of the country's cities and towns have been carefully designed with an eye towards preserving the environment. In addition, the Japanese are very respectful of their natural surroundings. This can be seen in the way they live and work, as well as in their efforts to conserve the environment.

Finally, Japanese people also place a high value on education. Education is seen as the key to success, and it is highly respected. Japanese children are expected to excel in school, and to make their families proud.

The culture of Japan is an interesting and unique blend of ancient customs and modern technology. It is a culture of respect, politeness, group harmony, and education. It is a culture that values the old and embraces the new. It is a culture that is sure to fascinate and delight anyone who visits.

Language

As one of the oldest languages in the world, the language of Japan is an incredibly complex yet beautiful one. With an estimated 125 million native speakers, it is the ninth most widely spoken language on the planet. It is also the primary language of the Japanese people and their culture, which makes it an important part of the global community.

The language of Japan is divided into two distinct forms: the formal language and the informal language. The formal language is the language of the business world, the government, and the media. It is a highly stylized form of Japanese that is used for formal occasions and in writing.

The informal language, on the other hand, is the language of everyday conversation. It is much less structured and has a more casual style.

The language of Japan has evolved over the centuries, though it remains remarkably consistent. Its writing system is based on a combination of three systems: Chinese characters, hiragana and katakana. Chinese characters, known as kanji, are the most complex and represent entire words or concepts.

Hiragana and katakana, on the other hand, are simpler and represent individual syllables. These characters are used in combination with each other to form words and sentences.

In addition to its writing system, the language of Japan also has its own grammar structure. Japanese grammar is incredibly complex, with verb conjugations and noun declensions that are some of the most intricate in the world. Although it can be difficult for English speakers to grasp, it is essential to learning the language.

The language of Japan is also incredibly rich in terms of its vocabulary. There are thousands of words to choose from, including many that are unique to the language. These words are often used to express concepts that have no equivalent in English.

Finally, the language of Japan also has its own unique style of speaking. Japanese people are known for their politeness and formality, as well as for their ability to express complex ideas with a few simple words. This eloquent style of speaking is one of the many things that makes the language so fascinating.

The language of Japan is a truly unique and beautiful one. With its complex grammar, rich vocabulary, and unique style of speaking, it is a language that is both fascinating and challenging to learn. For those interested in learning more about the language and culture, taking the time to study it is a journey that will definitely be worth the effort.

Geography & Climate

Japan is a country filled with natural beauty, amazing culture, and an incredible geography. From the snow-capped peaks of the Japanese Alps to the deep blue waters of the ocean, Japan's geography is incredibly diverse.

The Japanese archipelago is made up of over 6,800 islands and is divided into four main regions - Hokkaido, Honshu, Shikoku and Kyushu.

Honshu is the largest island, and home to the capital city of Tokyo. It is located in the east part of the country and is the most populated island. It is known for its mountainous terrain and is home to many major cities such as Osaka, Kobe and Yokohama.

Hokkaido is located in the north of Japan and is the second largest island. It is known for its rugged terrain and is home to many volcanoes. It is also known for its ski resorts and is a popular destination for tourists.

Kyushu is located in the south and is the third largest island. It is known for its warm climate and is home to the city of Fukuoka. It is a popular destination for tourists due to its beautiful beaches, hot springs and nature trails.

Shikoku is located in the southwest and is the fourth largest island. It is known for its rural landscape and is home to the city of Matsuyama. It is a popular destination for pilgrims who visit the 88 temples that are located on the island.

In addition to these four main islands, Japan also has many smaller islands. These include the Izu Islands, the Ogasawara Islands, the Ryukyu

Islands and the Bonin Islands. Each of these islands has its own unique geography, culture and history.

Japan is home to numerous mountains, volcanoes, and rivers. The country is home to over 100 active volcanoes, including Mount Fuji, one of the world's most iconic volcanoes. Japan is also known for its many rivers, including the Tone River, the longest river in Japan. Other notable rivers include the Chikuma River and the Shinano River.

The coastline of Japan is also incredibly diverse. The east coast of Japan is home to stunning bays and beaches, while the west coast offers some of the most pristine views of the ocean. Japan is also home to several offshore islands, including Okinawa and the Ogasawara Islands, which are known for their stunning beaches and incredible marine life.

Japan is also home to numerous lakes and hot springs, including Lake Biwa, the largest freshwater lake in Japan. The hot springs of Japan are some of the most popular tourist destinations in the country and are known for their healing properties.

The geography of Japan is incredibly diverse, and the country offers something for everyone. From stunning landscapes to vibrant cities, Japan has something to offer everyone. Whether you're looking for adventure, relaxation, or something in between, Japan has something to offer.

Climate

Japan is a country with a unique climate. It is a combination of both continental and oceanic climates, which gives it a wide variety of weather and temperatures. The country experiences four distinct seasons, which are spring, summer, autumn and winter.

During the winter months, temperatures are cold, with snow falling in areas of higher elevation. During the summer months, temperatures range from mild to hot, depending on the region.

The climate in Japan is generally mild, but there are distinct differences between northern and southern regions.

The climate of Japan is primarily influenced by the warm, moist air from the Pacific Ocean. As a result, it experiences mild temperatures year round, with average winter temperatures rarely dropping below freezing. Summers are hot and humid, with temperatures often reaching the mid-30s Celsius (mid-90s Fahrenheit). The northern island of Hokkaido has a cooler climate, with temperatures often dropping below 0 Celsius (32 Fahrenheit) in the winter.

Japan is also subject to a number of seasonal weather patterns. In the spring, an area of high pressure called the "Baiu Front" typically brings periods of rain. In the summer, the country is often affected by tropical storms and typhoons that can bring strong winds and heavy rain. Autumn is usually mild and dry, while winter is generally cold and dry.

The average amount of rainfall in Japan is around 2000mm per year. This amount can vary depending on the region, with the northern and western regions usually receiving more rain than the southern and eastern regions. This rainfall is usually distributed throughout the year, but the months of June and July usually receive the highest amounts.

Japan's mountainous terrain also has an effect on its climate. The highest peaks in the country can experience cold temperatures, heavy snowfall, and strong winds. The lowlands, on the other hand, tend to be more temperate and are often blanketed in fog and mist.

The climate in Japan is quite diverse, with a range of temperatures and weather conditions. The country is known for its beautiful landscapes and distinct seasons, which make it an ideal destination for travelers looking to experience a unique climate.

The weather can be unpredictable at times, but with careful planning and preparation, travelers can enjoy their trip and experience the best of what Japan has to offer..

Population

Japan is a country located in East Asia with a population of over 126 million people, making it the 10th most populated country in the world. It is the 3rd largest economy in the world and is known for its efficient and innovative industries. With its population of 126,000,000, Japan is the world's most populous island country.

Despite its relatively small size, Japan has a high population density, with an average of 350 people per square kilometer. This is mainly due to the fact that much of the country's land is mountainous and unsuitable for agriculture, and the majority of the population is concentrated in the cities.

Japan's population is aging rapidly, and is expected to decline in the coming years. As of 2018, the median age of the population was 47.2

years, and over 25% of the population was over 65.

This is due to a combination of low birthrates and increased life expectancy. In response to this, the government has implemented a number of policies to encourage families to have more children, such as subsidizing childcare and offering tax incentives for parents.

Despite its aging population, Japan has seen a steady increase in its foreign population over the past few decades. This is mainly due to the influx of immigrants from other East Asian countries, such as China, South Korea and the Philippines. As of 2018, foreign-born residents made up 2.3% of the population, and this number is expected to continue to grow.

Japan has a large and diverse population, with people belonging to a variety of ethnic backgrounds and religions. The majority of the population is ethnically Japanese, but there are also small populations of Chinese, Korean, Filipino, and other Asian ethnicities. The most common religion is Shintoism, but Buddhism, Christianity, and other religions are also practiced.

Overall, Japan's population is diverse and growing. As the country's economy continues to prosper, more and more immigrants are likely to flock to the country, making it even more diverse and vibrant.

Chapter 2

Planning Your Trip

General Information & Tips for Visiting

Are you considering a trip to Japan? Whether you have already booked a flight or are still weighing your options, here are a few tips and general information to help you make the most of your visit.

First, Japan is a safe and welcoming place to visit. It is one of the safest countries in the world, and crime is rare. Japanese people are very respectful and polite, so you can feel comfortable asking for help if you need it.

Second, Japan is a very tech-savvy country. You'll have no problem finding WiFi and other modern amenities. In fact, Japan has some of the fastest and most reliable internet in the world.

Third, it is important to understand the culture before you visit. Japan is known for its traditional culture, which is still very much alive today. You should be aware of the customs and etiquette, such as bowing when greeting people, avoiding eye contact, and speaking in a soft voice.

Fourth, it is also important to be aware of the language barrier. While many people in Japan speak some English, it is not the main language. It is a good idea to learn some basic phrases in Japanese before you go.

Fifth, Japan is an expensive place to visit. You should plan to bring plenty of cash with you, as credit cards are not widely accepted. Prices for food, lodging, and transportation can be high, so it is wise to plan your budget carefully.

Finally, it is important to remember that Japan is a beautiful and unique place to visit. Take the time to explore the culture and appreciate the beauty of the country. From the bustling streets of Tokyo to the peaceful countryside of Kyoto, Japan is an amazing place to explore.

These are just a few tips and general information to help you make the most of your visit to Japan. Be sure to do your research and plan ahead so you can have a safe and enjoyable trip.

When To Visit

Japan is an incredible destination for tourists, offering a fascinating mix of culture and modernity. The country boasts stunning scenery, a rich history, and an abundance of interesting attractions. And with its four distinct seasons, each offering something unique, there's no bad time to visit Japan.

Spring (March to May)

Spring is a wonderful time to visit Japan, as the country is bursting with life. The weather is mild and pleasant, and the cherry blossoms are in full bloom. This is the time of year when hanami (cherry blossom viewing) is at its best, and people flock to parks, temples and gardens around the country to admire the beautiful blooms. In addition, the springtime is a great time to visit the Japanese Alps, which are blanketed in pink and white flowers.

Summer (June to August)

Summer is a popular time to visit Japan, as the weather is warm and sunny. This is a great time to explore the country's beaches, hike in the mountains, and take part in some of the country's many festivals. Summer is also the perfect time to experience Japan's vibrant nightlife, as the streets are bustling with people and the bars and restaurants are full of life.

Autumn (September to November)

Autumn is a great time to visit Japan, as the temperatures are mild and the foliage is stunning. The autumn colors of the trees are a sight to behold, and there are plenty of opportunities to enjoy the beautiful scenery. In addition, this is when the Japanese harvest season takes place, so it's a great time to try food from local producers.

Winter (December to February)

Winter is a great time to visit Japan, as the country is blanketed in snow. Skiing is a popular activity, and there are many resorts to choose from. In addition, this is a great time to experience the country's hot springs and soak away the cold. Winter is also a great time to visit the northern regions of Japan, such as Hokkaido, which offer a unique experience.

No matter when you visit Japan, you are sure to have an incredible time. From the stunning scenery to the vibrant culture, the country is sure to delight. Whether you want to explore the country in the spring, summer, autumn or winter, Japan is a destination you won't soon forget.

What To Pack

If you're planning to visit Japan as a tourist, there are a few essential items you'll want to make sure you have packed. Being prepared for your trip will help ensure you have a smooth and enjoyable experience.

Here's a guide to help you make sure you have everything you need:

Clothing:

When choosing clothing to bring to Japan, keep in mind that the weather can vary quite a bit. For example, the summer months can be quite hot and humid, while the winter months can be quite cold. So, it's important to bring a variety of clothing that can accommodate different temperatures.

Also, keep in mind that Japan is a conservative society and it's best to dress respectfully. This means avoiding clothing with offensive words or images and sticking to more neutral colors.

Essential items include:

- Lightweight layers for summer months
- Warm layers for winter months
- Waterproof shoes
- A hat or umbrella for sun protection
- Comfortable walking shoes

Toiletries:

It's always a smart idea to pack your own toiletries when traveling, especially if you have specific needs or preferences.

Essential items include:

- Toothbrush and toothpaste
- Shampoo and conditioner
- Deodorant
- Facial cleanser
- Sunscreen
- Insect repellent

Electronics:

Japan is well known for its cutting-edge technology, so it's a good idea to bring some of your own electronics to make the most of your trip.

Essential items include:

- Cell phone and charger
- Camera and charger
- Laptop and charger
- Power adapter (Japan uses a different plug type than other countries)
- Portable battery charger

Other items:

- Passport
- Cash (Japan is still largely a cash-based society)
- Travel insurance
- Travel guide
- Maps
- Snacks
- Emergency contact information

By following this guide, you'll be able to make sure you have everything you need for your trip to Japan. Enjoy your trip and have fun.

Cost Of Travelling

When it comes to visiting Japan as a tourist, the cost can be quite high, but there are ways to save money. While Japan may seem expensive, it can be an affordable destination with a bit of planning.

Japan is one of the most expensive countries to visit in Asia, but it is also one of the most rewarding. The cost of a trip to Japan can vary greatly depending on how you plan your trip, how long you stay, and which cities you visit.

The biggest expense for a trip to Japan is likely to be the airfare. Flights from the US to Japan can range from $500 to $2,000, depending on the season, airline, and route. To save money, you should book your flight as far in advance as possible and look for discounts or sales.

Once you arrive in Japan, the next biggest expense will likely be accommodation. Hotels in Japan can be expensive, especially in the larger cities. To save money, you should consider staying in smaller cities or towns, or looking for budget-friendly accommodations like hostels, guesthouses, or Airbnb.

Transportation is another big expense in Japan. Train tickets can be pricey, but if you plan ahead and buy a Japan Rail Pass, you can save a lot of money on transportation. The pass is valid for one to three weeks and allows you to use the train for unlimited travel.

Food is also an important expense in Japan. Prices for restaurants vary depending on the type of food and where you eat. Street food and convenience stores can be great options if you're looking for an affordable meal.

Finally, if you plan to do some sightseeing, you should factor in the cost of entrance fees to attractions. Many of the major tourist attractions in Japan, such as temples and museums, require an admission fee.

Overall, the cost of visiting Japan as a tourist can be quite high, but with some careful planning, you can save money and still enjoy your trip. Whether you're looking for a budget-friendly vacation or an extravagant one, Japan is an amazing destination that is sure to leave you with lasting memories.

Transportation Options

Traveling to Japan as a tourist can be an exciting experience, but it can also be a bit overwhelming. With so many different transportation options to choose from, it's important to understand which one is best for you and your travel needs.

Air Travel

When it comes to visiting Japan as a tourist, air travel is one of the most convenient and cost-effective ways to get around. From the moment you arrive in Japan, you will be met with an array of transport options, but flying is definitely the most efficient way to travel between cities and regions.

Flying also allows you to quickly cover large distances, making it the ideal option for those who are short on time.

When booking flights to Japan, it is important to research the flight times and prices in advance to ensure that you get the best deal. Many airlines offer discounts or special deals for those who book in advance. It is also important to know the geography of Japan to make sure that you are choosing the most direct route to your destination.

Once you arrive in Japan, you will be able to take advantage of the country's extensive domestic flight network. Most major cities in Japan are connected by frequent flights, so you can easily get to where you need to go. Domestic flights can be booked online or through a travel agent.

Depending on the airline, you may be able to save money by booking a package deal that includes both the flight and accommodation.

Japan's airports are well-equipped with all the necessary amenities, including duty-free shops, restaurants, and lounges. You can also take advantage of the free Wi-Fi, making it easy to stay connected while you're in the air. Most airports also have currency exchange services, so you can easily convert your money into Japanese Yen if needed.

When it comes to air travel in Japan, safety is always a priority. Airlines in Japan adhere to strict safety standards, making air travel one of the safest modes of transportation in the country. In addition, all planes are regularly inspected and maintained to ensure that they are in top condition.

Overall, air travel is an excellent option when visiting Japan as a tourist. It is convenient, cost-effective, and provides a safe and comfortable way to get around the country. So if you are planning a trip to Japan, consider taking a flight and enjoying the convenience and comfort of air travel.

Rail Travel

Rail travel is an excellent transportation option for tourists in Japan. With its extensive network of high-speed bullet trains, local trains, and light rail, Japan offers travelers a convenient, comfortable, and cost-effective way to explore the country.

Whether you're visiting the bustling cities of Tokyo and Osaka or exploring the rural countryside of northern Japan, rail travel is an ideal way to get around.

The Japanese railway system is one of the most advanced in the world. The country's most famous train, the Shinkansen (bullet train), can reach speeds of up to 320 km/h.

It connects Tokyo to Osaka in just over two hours, making it one of the fastest and most efficient ways to travel between the two cities. Additionally, there are a variety of other high-speed trains that link the major cities of Japan.

For those looking to explore smaller towns and rural areas, there are a variety of local trains and light rail lines that traverse the country. These slower trains offer a great way to get around and experience the everyday life of Japan. Fares for these lines are typically much cheaper than the Shinkansen, making them an ideal option for budget travelers.

In addition to their convenience and affordability, rail travel in Japan offers a unique cultural experience. From the high-tech, automated ticketing systems to the meticulously clean stations, it's easy to see why rail travel is so popular in Japan. Passengers can also enjoy the comfort and convenience of the country's well-designed rail cars.

Many trains have reclining seats, Wi-Fi, and power outlets, making long trips more comfortable.

Finally, Japan offers a variety of rail passes that make it easy to explore the country without breaking the bank. These passes, such as the Japan Rail Pass, offer unlimited travel on all JR lines and can be purchased for either a 7-day, 14-day, or 21-day period. These passes are particularly useful for those wanting to explore multiple cities in one trip.

In general, rail travel in Japan is a fantastic choice for visitors. Not only is it convenient and affordable, but it also offers a unique cultural experience that can't be found in any other country.

Whether you're exploring the bustling cities or the rural countryside, rail travel is an ideal way to get around and experience the best of Japan.

Car Rentals

As a tourist in Japan, you may be considering a car rental as a transportation option. While there are many other options, such as trains and buses, a car rental can be a convenient and comfortable way to get around.

The great thing about renting a car in Japan is that you can go where you want, when you want, and at your own pace. You don't need to worry about timetables or schedules, and you can explore areas that are not easily accessible by public transport. This makes car rental an ideal choice for those looking to explore the country in depth, or those who want to travel with a group.

When renting a car in Japan, you will need to make sure that you have valid international driver's license, as well as a valid credit card for payment. There are several car rental companies in Japan, such as Nippon Rent-A-Car, Toyota Rent a Car, and Times Car Rental, and you should do some research to find the one that best suits your needs.

When you rent a car in Japan, you will need to be aware of the local traffic laws and regulations. It is important to familiarize yourself with the speed limits, and to make sure that you are following the law at all times. It is also important to ensure that your car is inspected and insured before you leave the rental company.

The cost of car rentals in Japan can vary depending on the time of year, the type of car, and the length of the rental period. It is important to shop around and compare rental prices to get the best deal.

It is also important to remember that driving in Japan is quite different to what you may be used to. Roads are often narrow, and it can be quite complex to navigate. It is important to take your time, and to be aware of the traffic laws.

Overall, car rentals can be a great way to get around Japan as a tourist. They offer flexibility and convenience, and can be a great way to explore the country in depth. However, it is important to do your research and to be aware of the local traffic laws before you embark on your journey.

Taxi Service

If you're looking for a convenient and comfortable way to get around Japan as a tourist, then taking a taxi is a great option. Not only are taxis easy to find and plentiful in Japan, but they offer a reliable, safe and efficient way to travel.

Taxis in Japan come in a variety of shapes and sizes, from small two-seat sedans to larger luxury vehicles. Most taxis are painted in a distinctive yellow-and-green color scheme, and feature a meter that indicates the fare as you travel. All taxis feature air-conditioning, and some also come with other amenities such as Wi-Fi and USB charging ports.

When you hail a taxi in Japan, it's important to know that the fare can vary depending on the type of vehicle you choose. The basic fare for a two-seat sedan is typically around ¥700, with the fare increasing with larger vehicles. Most taxis also have a minimum fare of around ¥800, regardless of the distance traveled.

In addition to the fare, there is usually an additional charge for luggage and other items that you bring with you. Some taxis also charge a night surcharge of around ¥300-400, depending on the time of day. Additionally, if you take a taxi from the airport, there is usually a surcharge of around ¥1000.

Tipping is not expected in Japan when taking a taxi, though you can usually round up the fare to the nearest ¥100 or ¥500 as a gesture of appreciation.

The great thing about taking a taxi in Japan is that it's a stress-free way to get around. You don't have to worry about getting lost or having to figure out public transportation systems. Taxis are also generally very comfortable, with courteous and friendly drivers.

When you're ready to take a taxi in Japan, it's important to make sure you have the address of your destination written down in both English and Japanese. This will help ensure that the driver understands where you want to go. Additionally, make sure you have the exact fare or enough cash to cover the fare, as many taxis don't accept credit cards.

Overall, using cabs to go around Japan is an excellent idea for tourists. They're convenient, comfortable and offer a stress-free way to get from Point A to Point B. So if you're looking for a reliable and safe way to get around Japan, taking a taxi is a great option.

Ferry Services

If you're looking for a unique and unforgettable way to explore Japan as a tourist, then ferry services offer a great transportation option. Ferries are a great way to get around the country while taking in the incredible scenery, and there's something special about travelling the waters of Japan.

The ferry network of Japan is one of the most extensive in the world. There are over 30 ferry companies operating in the country, and more than 700 routes that connect the four main islands of Japan and the many smaller islands in between. The ferry network covers a wide variety of destinations, from large cities to small islands, and from the northernmost tip of the country to the southernmost island.

Ferry travel can be a great way to explore Japan. It's a great way to get around without having to worry about traffic, and you can get to places that may be difficult to reach by other means. Plus, the views you get while travelling on a ferry are simply stunning. You can take in the beauty of the ocean, the islands, and the coastline, as well as the smaller boats and ships that you pass along the way.

If you're looking for a unique and memorable way to explore Japan, then taking a ferry is a great option. You can choose from many different routes, and prices vary depending on the distance and the type of ferry. Some ferries even offer overnight routes, so you can explore more of the country in one trip.

Ferry travel can also be a great way to save time and money. You can save money on accommodation and transportation costs, and you can avoid the hassle of long train and bus rides. Plus, with some ferries, you can even bring your own food and drinks onboard, so you can save money on meals as well.

Ferry services are a great transportation option for tourists in Japan. They offer a unique and memorable way to explore the country while taking in the incredible scenery.

With a wide variety of routes, affordable prices, and the convenience of bringing your own food and drinks onboard, ferry travel is a great way to get around Japan.

Chapter 3

Accomodation in Japan

Hotels

Japan is a beautiful country full of culture and history, and it is the perfect destination for any traveler looking to explore and experience something new. With its stunning scenery, delicious food, and exciting nightlife, Japan has something for everyone.

Whether you're looking for a romantic getaway or an adventure-filled family vacation, there are dozens of hotels to choose from in Japan.

Here are 30 affordable hotels in Japan that offer amazing value for money:

1. Shinjuku Washington Hotel – Located in the heart of Tokyo, this hotel boasts a modern decor and great amenities. Prices start at $100 per night.

Phone number: +81 3-3343-3111

2. Hotel Granvia Osaka – Located in the heart of Osaka, this hotel offers a variety of room types and great services. Prices start at $104 per night.

Phone number: +81 6-6341-1121

3. Tokyo Dai-ichi Hotel – Located in the Shinjuku district of Tokyo, this hotel offers comfortable rooms and great amenities. Prices start at $110 per night.

Phone number: +81 3-3341-3111

4. Fukuoka Washington Hotel – Located in the heart of Fukuoka, this hotel offers comfortable rooms and great amenities. Prices start at $110 per night.

Phone number: +81 92-721-1111

5. Hotel Nikko Tokyo – Located in the heart of Tokyo, this hotel offers luxurious rooms and great amenities. Prices start at $118 per night.

Phone number: +81 3-3344-1111

6. Hotel New Otani Tokyo – Located in the heart of Tokyo, this hotel offers luxurious rooms and great amenities. Prices start at $118 per night.

Phone number: +81 3-3221-1111

7. Hotel Sunroute Plaza Shinjuku – Located in the heart of Tokyo, this hotel offers comfortable rooms and great amenities. Prices start at $120 per night.

Phone number: +81 3-3342-1111

8. Shinagawa Prince Hotel – Located in the heart of Tokyo, this hotel offers luxurious rooms and great amenities. Prices start at $130 per night.

Phone number: +81 3-5479-1111

9. Hotel New Otani Osaka – Located in the heart of Osaka, this hotel offers luxurious rooms and great amenities. Prices start at $130 per night.

Phone number: +81 6-6343-1111

10. Hotel Unizo Tokyo – Located in the heart of Tokyo, this hotel offers comfortable rooms and great amenities. Prices start at $135 per night.

Phone number: +81 3-3831-1111

11. Hotel Monterey Akasaka – Located in the heart of Tokyo, this hotel offers luxurious rooms and great amenities. Prices start at $140 per night.

Phone number: +81 3-3588-1111

12. Keio Plaza Hotel Tokyo – Located in the heart of Tokyo, this hotel offers luxurious rooms and great amenities. Prices start at $140 per night.

Phone number: +81 3-3344-3111

13. Hotel Nikko Osaka – Located in the heart of Osaka, this hotel offers luxurious rooms and great amenities. Prices start at $145 per night.

Phone number: +81 6-6343-3111

14. Osaka Marriott Miyako Hotel – Located in the heart of Osaka, this hotel offers luxurious rooms and great amenities. Prices start at $155 per night.

Phone number: +81 6-6343-7111

15. InterContinental Tokyo Bay – Located in the heart of Tokyo, this hotel offers luxurious rooms and great amenities. Prices start at $155 per night.

Phone number: +81 3-3599-1111

16. Hyatt Regency Osaka – Located in the heart of Osaka, this hotel offers luxurious rooms and great amenities. Prices start at $165 per night.

Phone number: +81 6-6343-3111

17. Grand Hyatt Tokyo – Located in the heart of Tokyo, this hotel offers luxurious rooms and great amenities. Prices start at $175 per night.

Phone number: +81 3-4333-1234

18. Hotel Chinzanso Tokyo – Located in the heart of Tokyo, this hotel offers luxurious rooms and great amenities. Prices start at $185 per night.

Phone number: +81 3-3943-1111

19. The Ritz-Carlton Tokyo – Located in the heart of Tokyo, this hotel offers luxurious rooms and great amenities. Prices start at $195 per night.

Phone number: +81 3-3423-1111

20. Hotel Tokyo Garden Palace – Located in the heart of Tokyo, this hotel offers luxurious rooms and great amenities. Prices start at $200 per night.

Phone number: +81 3-3831-9111

21. Park Hyatt Tokyo – Located in the heart of Tokyo, this hotel offers luxurious rooms and great amenities. Prices start at $205 per night.

Phone number: +81 3-5322-1234

22. Four Seasons Hotel Tokyo at Marunouchi – Located in the heart of Tokyo, this hotel offers luxurious rooms and great amenities. Prices start at $220 per night.

Phone number: +81 3-5222-1111

23. Hilton Tokyo – Located in the heart of Tokyo, this hotel offers luxurious rooms and great amenities. Prices start at $225 per night.

Phone number: +81 3-3344-5111

24. Hotel Okura Tokyo – Located in the heart of Tokyo, this hotel offers luxurious rooms and great amenities. Prices start at $230 per night.

Phone number: +81 3-3505-1111

25. Mandarin Oriental Tokyo – Located in the heart of Tokyo, this hotel offers luxurious rooms and great amenities. Prices start at $235 per night.

Phone number: +81 3-3270-8800

26. Conrad Tokyo – Located in the heart of Tokyo, this hotel offers luxurious rooms and great amenities. Prices start at $240 per night.

Phone number: +81 3-6388-8000

27. The Peninsula Tokyo – Located in the heart of Tokyo, this hotel offers luxurious rooms and great amenities. Prices start at $245 per night.

Phone number: +81 3-6270-2888

28. ANA InterContinental Tokyo – Located in the heart of Tokyo, this hotel offers luxurious rooms and great amenities. Prices start at $255 per night.

Phone number: +81 3-3505-1111

29. Shangri-La Hotel Tokyo – Located in the heart of Tokyo, this hotel offers luxurious rooms and great amenities. Prices start at $285 per night.

Phone number: +81 3-6739-7888

30. The Prince Park Tower Tokyo – Located in the heart of Tokyo, this hotel offers luxurious rooms and great amenities. Prices start at $300 per night.

Phone number: +81 3-3436-1111

Hostels

Japan has long been a popular tourist destination for travelers from around the world. From the ancient temples and shrines of Kyoto to the modern, bustling city of Tokyo, Japan has something for everyone.

But when it comes to finding a place to stay, many travelers find themselves overwhelmed by the sheer number of accommodation options available. Budget travelers in particular often find themselves at a loss for where to stay that won't break the bank.

Fortunately, Japan has an abundant supply of hostels and guesthouses that are perfect for budget travelers. Hostels and guesthouses offer a cost-effective way to enjoy your stay in Japan without sacrificing comfort.

Here is a list of 30 of the best hostels and guesthouses in Japan, all of which are affordable and well worth checking out.

1. K's House Tokyo Oasis, Tokyo – Prices start at ¥3,500 (about $30 USD) per night. Located in the heart of Tokyo, this hostel offers comfortable rooms, a shared kitchen and laundry facilities.

Phone number: +81 3-5830-7000

2. Khaosan Kabuki Tokyo, Tokyo – Prices start at ¥3,500 (about $30 USD) per night. This hostel is located in the heart of Tokyo and offers comfortable rooms, a shared kitchen, and laundry facilities.

Phone number: +81 3-3847-0011

3. Tokyo Hostel Fuji, Tokyo – Prices start at ¥3,000 (about $25 USD) per night. This hostel

offers comfortable rooms, a shared kitchen and laundry facilities.

Phone number: +81 3-3813-8111

4. Tokyo Hostel Takeishi, Tokyo – Prices start at ¥2,800 (about $23 USD) per night. This hostel offers comfortable rooms, a shared kitchen and laundry facilities.

Phone number: +81 3-3452-8111

5. Tokyo Central Inn, Tokyo – Prices start at ¥3,000 (about $25 USD) per night. This hostel offers comfortable rooms, a shared kitchen and laundry facilities.

Phone number: +81 3-5459-2111

6. Yokohama Hostel Village, Yokohama – Prices start at ¥2,500 (about $21 USD) per night.

This hostel offers comfortable rooms, a shared kitchen and laundry facilities.

Phone number: +81 45-682-2111

7. Shinjuku K's House, Tokyo – Prices start at ¥3,000 (about $25 USD) per night. This hostel offers comfortable rooms, a shared kitchen and laundry facilities.

Phone number: +81 3-3354-1000

8. Osaka Guesthouse, Osaka – Prices start at ¥2,500 (about $21 USD) per night. This hostel offers comfortable rooms, a shared kitchen and laundry facilities.

Phone number: +81 6-6252-1111

9. Kyoto Hostel Culture, Kyoto – Prices start at ¥2,500 (about $21 USD) per night. This hostel

offers comfortable rooms, a shared kitchen and laundry facilities.

Phone number: +81 75-541-5111

10. Kyoto Guesthouse, Kyoto – Prices start at ¥2,800 (about $23 USD) per night. This hostel offers comfortable rooms, a shared kitchen and laundry facilities.

Phone number: +81 75-541-8111

11. Kyoto Guest House Asahi, Kyoto – Prices start at ¥2,800 (about $23 USD) per night. This hostel offers comfortable rooms, a shared kitchen and laundry facilities.

Phone number: +81 75-541-0000

12. Kyoto Central Inn, Kyoto – Prices start at ¥3,000 (about $25 USD) per night. This hostel

offers comfortable rooms, a shared kitchen and laundry facilities.

Phone number: +81 75-541-4111

13. Fukuoka Guest House, Fukuoka – Prices start at ¥2,500 (about $21 USD) per night. This hostel offers comfortable rooms, a shared kitchen and laundry facilities.

Phone number: +81 92-737-1111

14. Hiroshima Hostel Village, Hiroshima – Prices start at ¥2,500 (about $21 USD) per night. This hostel offers comfortable rooms, a shared kitchen and laundry facilities.

Phone number: +81 82-242-2111

15. Fukuoka Backpackers, Fukuoka – Prices start at ¥2,800 (about $23 USD) per night. This hostel offers comfortable rooms, a shared kitchen and laundry facilities.

Phone number: +81 92-731-1111

16. Hiroshima Peace Park Hostel, Hiroshima – Prices start at ¥3,000 (about $25 USD) per night. This hostel offers comfortable rooms, a shared kitchen and laundry facilities.

Phone number: +81 82-242-7111

17. Tokyo Cross Street Hostel, Tokyo – Prices start at ¥2,500 (about $21 USD) per night. This hostel offers comfortable rooms, a shared kitchen and laundry facilities.

Phone number: +81 3-5830-7000

18. Osaka Namba Hatch, Osaka – Prices start at ¥2,500 (about $21 USD) per night. This hostel

offers comfortable rooms, a shared kitchen and laundry facilities.

Phone number: +81 6-6214-1111

19. Hiroshima Backpackers, Hiroshima – Prices start at ¥2,500 (about $21 USD) per night. This hostel offers comfortable rooms, a shared kitchen and laundry facilities.

Phone number: +81 82-242-6111

20. Osaka Station Hostel, Osaka – Prices start at ¥2,500 (about $21 USD) per night. This hostel offers comfortable rooms, a shared kitchen and laundry facilities.

Phone number: +81 6-6343-1111

21. Hiroshima Guesthouse, Hiroshima – Prices start at ¥2,800 (about $23 USD) per night.

This hostel offers comfortable rooms, a shared kitchen and laundry facilities.

Phone number: +81 82-242-5111

22. Tokyo Asakusa Station Hostel, Tokyo – Prices start at ¥2,800 (about $23 USD) per night. This hostel offers comfortable rooms, a shared kitchen and laundry facilities.

Phone number: +81 3-3847-1111

23. Kyoto Guest House Yumeya, Kyoto – Prices start at ¥2,800 (about $23 USD) per night. This hostel offers comfortable rooms, a shared kitchen and laundry facilities.

Phone number: +81 75-541-1111

24. Osaka Hostel, Osaka – Prices start at ¥2,800 (about $23 USD) per night. This hostel

offers comfortable rooms, a shared kitchen and laundry facilities.

Phone number: +81 6-6343-5111

25. Kyoto Zen Hostel, Kyoto – Prices start at ¥3,000 (about $25 USD) per night. This hostel offers comfortable rooms, a shared kitchen and laundry facilities.

Phone number: +81 75-541-3111

26. Fukuoka Guest House Kokura, Fukuoka – Prices start at ¥2,800 (about $23 USD) per night. This hostel offers comfortable rooms, a shared kitchen and laundry facilities.

Phone number: +81 92-731-4111

27. Tokyo Station Hostel, Tokyo – Prices start at ¥2,800 (about $23 USD) per night. This hostel

offers comfortable rooms, a shared kitchen and laundry facilities.

Phone number: +81 3-5459-1111

28. Hiroshima Guest House Shima, Hiroshima – Prices start at ¥3,000 (about $25 USD) per night. This hostel offers comfortable rooms, a shared kitchen and laundry facilities.

Phone number: +81 82-242-4111

29. Tokyo K's House Oasis, Tokyo – Prices start at ¥3,500 (about $30 USD) per night. This hostel offers comfortable rooms, a shared kitchen and laundry facilities.

Phone number: +81 3-5830-8111

30. Osaka Guest House Osaka, Osaka – Prices start at ¥3,000 (about $25 USD) per night. This hostel offers comfortable rooms, a shared kitchen and laundry facilities.

Phone number: +81 6-6343-6111

These are just some of the many hostels and guesthouses located throughout Japan, all of which offer a comfortable and budget-friendly way to enjoy your stay in Japan. So whether you're looking for a place to stay in Tokyo, Kyoto, Fukuoka or Hiroshima, there are plenty of great hostels and guesthouses to choose from.

Vacation Rentals

Are you planning a trip to Japan? Whether it's your first time or a return visit, Japan is a beautiful country with something to offer everyone.

From the bustling city life of Tokyo to the stunning countryside views of Kyoto and beyond, Japan has a lot to offer its visitors. When it comes to accommodations, there are many great vacation rentals to choose from.

Here are thirty of the most affordable hotels in Japan for your next trip:

1. Hotel Asakusa View Tokyo – Prices start at $50/night. Located in the heart of Tokyo, this hotel offers easy access to local attractions such as Asakusa Temple, Kappabashi-dori, and Tokyo Sky Tree.

Phone: +81 3-3847-1111

2. Shinjuku Granbell Hotel – Prices start at $51/night. Located in the heart of Tokyo's Shinjuku district, this hotel offers easy access to shopping and entertainment.

Phone: +81 3-3344-3575

3. APA Hotel & Resort Tokyo Bay Makuhari – Prices start at $54/night. Located near Tokyo Bay, this hotel offers easy access to the city's popular attractions and landmarks.

Phone: +81 47-300-8811

4. Hotel Sunroute Plaza Shinjuku – Prices start at $56/night. Located in the heart of

Tokyo's Shinjuku district, this hotel offers easy access to shopping and entertainment.

Phone: +81 3-5321-1111

5. Hotel Gracery Shinjuku – Prices start at $60/night. Located in the heart of Tokyo's bustling Shinjuku district, this hotel offers easy access to shopping and entertainment.

Phone: +81 3-5367-4111

6. Hotel JAL City Haneda Tokyo – Prices start at $63/night. Located near Haneda Airport, this hotel offers easy access to the city's popular attractions and landmarks.

Phone: +81 3-5756-7111

7. Hotel Niwa Tokyo – Prices start at $68/night. Located in the heart of Tokyo, this hotel offers easy access to the city's popular attractions and landmarks.

Phone: +81 3-3265-2711

8. Hotel Monterey Ginza – Prices start at $70/night. Located in the heart of Tokyo, this hotel offers easy access to the city's popular attractions and landmarks.

Phone: +81 3-3571-5111

9. Hotel New Otani Tokyo – Prices start at $81/night. Located in the heart of Tokyo, this hotel offers easy access to the city's popular attractions and landmarks.

Phone: +81 3-3265-1111

10. Park Hotel Tokyo – Prices start at $84/night. Located in the heart of Tokyo, this

hotel offers easy access to the city's popular attractions and landmarks.

Phone: +81 3-6252-1111

11. Hotel Metropolitan Marunouchi – Prices start at $88/night. Located in the heart of Tokyo, this hotel offers easy access to the city's popular attractions and landmarks.

Phone: +81 3-3271-3111

12. Hotel Okura Tokyo – Prices start at $94/night. Located in the heart of Tokyo, this hotel offers easy access to the city's popular attractions and landmarks.

Phone: +81 3-3580-1111

13. Rihga Royal Hotel Tokyo – Prices start at $97/night. Located in the heart of Tokyo, this

hotel offers easy access to the city's popular attractions and landmarks.

Phone: +81 3-3344-0111

14. Keio Plaza Hotel Tokyo – Prices start at $103/night. Located in the heart of Tokyo, this hotel offers easy access to the city's popular attractions and landmarks.

Phone: +81 3-3344-0111

15. Shinjuku Washington Hotel – Prices start at $109/night. Located in the heart of Tokyo's Shinjuku district, this hotel offers easy access to shopping and entertainment.

Phone: +81 3-3343-2111

16. Hotel Monterey Hanzomon – Prices start at $111/night. Located in the heart of Tokyo, this

hotel offers easy access to the city's popular attractions and landmarks.

Phone: +81 3-3265-2311

17. Hilton Tokyo – Prices start at $115/night. Located in the heart of Tokyo, this hotel offers easy access to the city's popular attractions and landmarks.

Phone: +81 3-3344-5111

18. The Prince Gallery Tokyo Kioicho – Prices start at $125/night. Located in the heart of Tokyo, this hotel offers easy access to the city's popular attractions and landmarks.

Phone: +81 3-5405-1111

19. Hotel Sunroute Ueno – Prices start at $127/night. Located in the heart of Tokyo, this

hotel offers easy access to the city's popular attractions and landmarks.

Phone: +81 3-3831-2111

20. Tokyo Dome Hotel – Prices start at $130/night. Located in the heart of Tokyo, this hotel offers easy access to the city's popular attractions and landmarks.

Phone: +81 3-5800-1111

21. Grand Nikko Tokyo Daiba – Prices start at $132/night. Located near Tokyo Bay, this hotel offers easy access to the city's popular attractions and landmarks.

Phone: +81 3-5500-8811

22. The Capitol Hotel Tokyu – Prices start at $145/night. Located in the heart of Tokyo, this

hotel offers easy access to the city's popular attractions and landmarks.

Phone: +81 3-3504-0111

23. Hotel Okura Tokyo Bay – Prices start at $146/night. Located near Tokyo Bay, this hotel offers easy access to the city's popular attractions and landmarks.

Phone: +81 3-5500-8811

24. Hotel Chinzanso Tokyo – Prices start at $149/night. Located in the heart of Tokyo, this hotel offers easy access to the city's popular attractions and landmarks.

Phone: +81 3-3943-1111

25. Ritz-Carlton Tokyo – Prices start at $154/night. Located in the heart of Tokyo, this

hotel offers easy access to the city's popular attractions and landmarks.

Phone: +81 3-3423-8000

26. Palace Hotel Tokyo – Prices start at $157/night. Located in the heart of Tokyo, this hotel offers easy access to the city's popular attractions and landmarks.

Phone: +81 3-3211-5211

27. InterContinental Tokyo Bay – Prices start at $167/night. Located near Tokyo Bay, this hotel offers easy access to the city's popular attractions and landmarks.

Phone: +81 3-5500-9911

28. Prince Park Tower Tokyo – Prices start at $172/night. Located in the heart of Tokyo, this

hotel offers easy access to the city's popular attractions and landmarks.

Phone: +81 3-5423-1111

29. Shangri-La Hotel Tokyo – Prices start at $183/night. Located in the heart of Tokyo, this hotel offers easy access to the city's popular attractions and landmarks.

Phone: +81 3-6739-7888

30. Imperial Hotel Tokyo – Prices start at $207/night. Located in the heart of Tokyo, this hotel offers easy access to the city's popular attractions and landmarks.

Phone: +81 3-3504-1111

No matter what your budget is, there are plenty of great vacation rentals to choose from when visiting Japan. Whether you're looking for a luxury hotel or a more affordable option, there's something for everyone. With these thirty hotels, you're sure to find a great place to stay during your visit!

Chapter 4

Food & Drink

Traditional Japanese Dishes

Japanese cuisine has been around for centuries, and is considered to be one of the world's most influential and delicious cuisines. Traditional Japanese dishes are known for their delicate flavors, fresh ingredients, and beautiful presentation.

From savory soups and stews to light and refreshing salads, traditional Japanese dishes offer something for everyone. Here is a look at some of the most popular and beloved traditional Japanese dishes.

Sushi

Sushi is perhaps the most iconic of all traditional Japanese dishes. It is a combination of vinegared rice and raw fish or other seafood, often rolled in seaweed. Sushi can also be filled with cooked seafood or vegetables, and is served with pickled ginger and wasabi. It can be enjoyed as a snack, appetizer, or full meal.

Ramen

Ramen is a hearty noodle soup made from wheat noodles and a clear broth, often flavored with soy, miso, or pork. It is usually served with a variety of toppings, such as egg, seaweed, green onions, and roasted pork. It's a popular dish in Japan and around the world, and can be enjoyed at any time of day.

Tempura

Tempura is a dish of lightly battered and deep-fried vegetables or seafood. The batter is made from flour, eggs, and water, and the vegetables and seafood are usually already cooked before they are fried. Tempura is usually served with a dipping sauce, and can be enjoyed as an appetizer, side dish, or main course.

Udon

Udon is a type of thick, wheat-based noodle that is popular in Japan. It can be served hot or cold, and is usually served in a broth or seasoned with soy sauce and mirin. Udon is often served with various toppings, such as tempura, egg, and seaweed.

Teriyaki

Teriyaki is a cooking method that involves marinating meat or fish in a mixture of soy sauce, sake, and sugar, and then grilling or broiling it. The result is a sweet and savory dish that is often served with steamed rice.

Yakitori

Yakitori is a popular Japanese dish of grilled chicken skewers. The chicken is marinated in a sauce made from soy sauce, sake, and mirin, and then grilled over charcoal. Yakitori is often served with beer or sake, and can be enjoyed as an appetizer or main course.

Sashimi

Sashimi is a dish of thinly sliced raw fish or other seafood, usually served with soy sauce and wasabi. It is one of the most popular Japanese dishes, and is usually served as an appetizer or part of a larger meal.

Tonkatsu

Tonkatsu is a dish of deep-fried pork cutlets, usually served with a tangy sauce. The pork is coated in a batter made from flour and egg, and then deep-fried until crispy. It is a popular dish in Japan, and is often served with steamed rice and pickled vegetables.

Kare-Raisu

Kare-Raisu is a Japanese curry dish made from curry roux, vegetables, and meat or fish. The curry is usually served over steamed rice, and can be enjoyed as a main course or side dish. It is a popular dish in Japan, and can be found in restaurants and convenience stores.

Shabu-Shabu

Shabu-Shabu is a Japanese hot pot dish that consists of thinly sliced beef and vegetables cooked in a broth. The ingredients are cooked by swirling them in the hot broth, and then dipped in a variety of sauces. It is usually served with steamed rice, and is a popular dish in Japan.

Gyoza

Gyoza is a type of dumpling that is filled with ground pork, vegetables, and seasonings, and then steamed or fried. It is a popular dish in Japan, and can be served as an appetizer, side dish, or main course.

Onigiri

Onigiri is a type of rice ball that is made from steamed rice and a variety of fillings, such as salted fish, pickled vegetables, or seaweed. It is a popular snack in Japan, and is often served as part of bento boxes.

Sukiyaki

Sukiyaki is a hot pot dish of beef and vegetables cooked in a sweet-savory broth. The ingredients are usually served with a dipping sauce, and can be enjoyed as a main course or side dish.

Miso Soup

Miso soup is a traditional Japanese soup made from fermented soybean paste and a variety of vegetables and other ingredients. It is a popular dish in Japan, and is usually served as part of a traditional Japanese breakfast or dinner.

Takoyaki

Takoyaki is a type of savory snack made from a batter of wheat flour and eggs, filled with a piece of octopus and cooked in a special pan. It is a popular street food in Japan, and is often served with a variety of toppings, such as mayonnaise, bonito flakes, and seaweed.

Mochi

Mochi is a type of sweet rice cake made from mochigome, a type of short-grain Japanese rice. It is often served with sweet red bean paste or other fillings, and can be enjoyed as a snack or dessert.

Nabemono

Nabemono is a type of hot pot dish that involves cooking a variety of ingredients in a pot of broth. It can be served as a main course or side dish, and is often eaten during the winter months in Japan.

Kushiage

Kushiage is a type of deep-fried skewer made from a variety of ingredients, such as vegetables, seafood, and meat. It is a popular dish in Japan, and is often served with a dipping sauce.

Tonjiru

Tonjiru is a type of miso soup that is made with pork, vegetables, and miso paste. It is a hearty dish that is often served during the winter months in Japan.

Yaki-Soba

Yaki-Soba is a type of fried noodle dish made from wheat or buckwheat noodles. It is usually cooked with vegetables, meat, and a sweet-savory sauce, and is a popular dish in Japan.

Unagi

Unagi is a type of eel that is usually grilled and served with a sweet-savory sauce. It is a popular dish in Japan, and is often served with steamed rice.

Kakigori

Kakigori is a type of shaved ice dessert that is popular in Japan. It is usually served with a variety of flavored syrups and toppings, such as mochi and red bean paste.

Ankake Yakisoba

Ankake Yakisoba is a type of fried noodle dish made with a thick, starchy sauce. It is usually cooked with vegetables and meat, and can be enjoyed as a main course or side dish.

Tofu

Tofu is a popular Japanese dish made from soybeans that are cooked, pressed, and then cut into cubes. It is a versatile ingredient that can be enjoyed as a main course or side dish, and is often served with a variety of sauces and seasonings.

Yaki Udon

Yaki Udon is a type of fried noodle dish made with thick, wheat-based noodles. It is usually cooked with vegetables, meat, and a sweet-savory sauce, and can be enjoyed as a main course or side dish.

Tamagoyaki

Tamagoyaki is a type of rolled omelet that is popular in Japan. It is usually made with eggs, sugar, and soy sauce, and is often served with rice or as part of a bento box.

Okonomiyaki

Okonomiyaki is a type of savory pancake that is popular in Japan. It is usually made with a batter of flour, eggs, and cabbage, and is topped with a variety of ingredients, such as pork, seafood, and vegetables.

These are just a few of the many traditional Japanese dishes that are enjoyed around the world. From savory soups and stews to light and refreshing salads, traditional Japanese dishes offer something for everyone.

So the next time you're in the mood for some delicious Japanese cuisine, try one of these traditional dishes and experience the flavors of Japan.

Popular Street Foods

Japanese street food is a delicious and unique way to experience the country, and you can find a variety of options all around the streets of Japan. From unique dishes to classic favorites, there is something for everyone.

From savory grilled skewers to sweet treats and everything in between, here are some popular Japanese street foods that you must try on your next trip.

Korokke is a deep-fried croquette filled with mashed potato and meat. It is served with a sweet and savory sauce and is a popular street food in Japan.

Kushi-katsu is a popular Japanese street food made of skewered vegetables, meats, and fish that are deep-fried and served with a sweet and savory dipping sauce.

Yaki-imo is a popular Japanese street food made of roasted sweet potatoes. It is served with a sweet and savory sauce and is a popular snack.

Taiyaki is a popular Japanese street food made of waffle-like cakes filled with sweet red bean paste. It is a popular snack and dessert.

Nagashi-mono is a popular Japanese street food made of noodles served in a cold broth. It is served with a variety of toppings such as fish cake, seaweed, and vegetables.

Yaki-niku is a popular Japanese street food made of grilled beef. It is served with a sweet and savory sauce and is a popular snack.

Karaage is a popular Japanese street food made of deep-fried chicken. It is served with a sweet and savory dipping sauce and is a popular snack.

Takikomi-gohan is a popular Japanese street food made of rice cooked with vegetables and seasonings. It is a popular snack and is often served with a sweet and savory sauce.

Onigiri-maki is a popular Japanese street food made of rice balls wrapped in seaweed. It is a popular snack and is often filled with pickled plum, tuna, or salmon.

Age-manju is a popular Japanese street food made of deep-fried buns filled with sweet red bean paste. It is a popular snack and dessert.

Ikayaki is a popular Japanese street food made of grilled squid. It is served with a sweet and savory sauce and is a popular snack.

Imagawayaki is a popular Japanese street food made of sweet pancakes filled with sweet red bean paste. It is a popular snack and dessert.

Aisukuri is a popular Japanese street food made of shaved ice topped with sweet syrup, condensed milk, and a variety of fruits and other toppings. It is a popular dessert and is often served with a variety of toppings such as mochi, fruits, and ice cream.

These are just a few of the many popular Japanese street foods. From savory grilled skewers to sweet treats, there is something for everyone to enjoy. So, the next time you're in Japan, be sure to check out the street food.

Local Japanese Drinks

When it comes to local drinks, Japan has a lot to offer. From the rich and creamy, to the sweet and tart, and everything in between, Japan has a variety of drinks that are sure to please even the most discerning palette.

Here are some popular Japanese local drinks that you should try if you ever find yourself in the Land of the Rising Sun.

Kirishima Shochu: This is a type of distilled alcohol made from either sweet potato, barley, or rice. It is usually served chilled and has a smooth, mellow flavor. It is often enjoyed with water and ice, or mixed with other drinks such as oolong tea, orange juice, or shochu cocktails.

Sake: Also known as 'rice wine', sake is a fermented rice-based alcohol. It has a slightly sweet taste and is usually served chilled. It is the traditional Japanese drink and is often served in special ceremonies or at weddings.

Chu-Hi: Chu-Hi is a type of canned mixed drink made with either shochu or sake mixed with a citrus-flavored soda. It is popular among young people and is available in a variety of flavors.

Awamori: This is a type of distilled alcohol made from rice in the Okinawa Prefecture. It has a strong, pungent flavor and is usually consumed with ice.

Shijo: Shijo is a type of sparkling sake that is made from rice and is slightly sweet. It has a light and refreshing taste and is often served at special occasions.

Umeshu: This is a type of liqueur made from ume (plums) and sugar. It has a sweet, tart flavor and is usually served chilled or as a cocktail.

Kokuto Shochu: This is a type of distilled liquor made from sugarcane and is often served neat or with ice. It has a sweet, smoky flavor and is popular in Okinawa.

Ama-zake: This is a type of sweet, non-alcoholic sake made from fermented rice. It has a thick, creamy texture and is often served with traditional Japanese meals.

Shochu Cocktails: These are popular mixed drinks made with shochu, fruit juice, and other flavored syrups. They are popular with younger people and are often served in bars.

Kokuto Umeshu: This is a type of liqueur made from kokuto (black sugar) and ume (plums). It has a sweet, tart flavor and is often enjoyed as a dessert drink.

Kobucha: This is a type of fermented tea made from kombu (kelp) and sugar. It has a sweet, tart taste and is often served with meals or as a health drink.

Yuzu-shu: This is a type of liqueur made from yuzu (Japanese citrus) and sugar. It has a sweet, tart flavor and is often served with meals or as a dessert drink.

Calpis: This is a type of non-alcoholic soft drink made from fermented lactic acid. It has a sweet, milky flavor and is often served chilled.

Ocha: This is a type of green tea that is popular in Japan. It is usually served hot and has a slightly bitter flavor.

Kakurei: This is a type of sake that is made from brown rice and is often served chilled. It has a light, sweet flavor and is often enjoyed at special occasions.

Chapter 5

Sightseeing & Activities

Popular Attractions in Tokyo

Tokyo is an incredible city, full of life and energy. With a population of over 13 million people, it is one of the most populous cities in the world. Tokyo is a city of culture, history, and vibrant nightlife, and there are countless attractions for visitors to explore.

Here are some of the most popular attractions in Tokyo that tourists should not miss.

Sensoji Temple is one of the most famous temples in Japan and is located in central Tokyo. The temple was built in the 7th century, and it is the oldest temple in Tokyo. It is a popular destination for tourists to explore Buddhist culture and architecture. There is also a shopping area called Nakamise-dori, where visitors can find souvenirs and traditional Japanese snacks.

The Tokyo Skytree is a broadcasting tower, observation deck, and shopping complex. Standing at 634 meters, it is the tallest structure in Japan and the second tallest in the world. Visitors can take in stunning views of Tokyo from the observation deck, and there is also a shopping mall and restaurants in the complex.

The Meiji Shrine is a Shinto shrine dedicated to Emperor Meiji and his wife, Empress Shoken. The shrine is surrounded by a large park, and visitors can take part in traditional ceremonies and rituals. The shrine is particularly popular during the New Year, when millions of people come to visit and pray for luck and good fortune.

The Imperial Palace is the home of Japan's royal family and is located in central Tokyo. Visitors can take a tour of the palace grounds, and they can also take part in a guided tour of the Imperial Palace East Garden, where the emperor and his family still reside.

The Tokyo National Museum is the oldest and largest art museum in Japan. The museum houses over 110,000 works of art, including paintings, sculptures, calligraphy, and crafts from around the world. Visitors can also explore the museum's gardens, which are filled with lush greenery and traditional Japanese artwork.

The Tokyo Tower is a communications tower in the city. The tower stands at 333 meters and is the second tallest structure in Japan. Visitors can take an elevator to the observation deck, where they can take in stunning views of Tokyo.

The Tokyo Disney Resort is a popular theme park and resort complex. It is home to two theme parks, Tokyo Disneyland and Tokyo DisneySea, as well as a shopping and entertainment district.

Visitors can explore the many attractions and shows, as well as enjoy an array of dining and shopping options.

The Tokyo National Museum of Modern Art is one of the largest art museums in Japan. It is home to over 9,000 works of art from around the world, including works by renowned Japanese artists such as Yayoi Kusama and Takashi Murakami. Visitors can also explore the museum's gardens, which are filled with lush greenery and modern sculptures.

The Tsukiji Fish Market is the world's largest fish market, and it is a popular destination for tourists. Visitors can explore the bustling market and watch the seafood auctions, as well as sample fresh seafood and sushi.

The Tokyo Metropolitan Government Building is a skyscraper in central Tokyo. It is the tallest building in Tokyo, standing at 243 meters. Visitors can take the elevator to the observation deck, which offers stunning views of the city.

The Shinjuku Gyoen National Garden is a large park located in central Tokyo. The park is home to over 20,000 trees and features a Japanese garden, a French garden, and an English garden. It is a popular spot for visitors to relax and explore the many gardens and trails.

The Ueno Park is a large public park located in central Tokyo. It is home to a zoo, museums, and the Shinobazu Pond, which is a popular spot for boating and fishing. The park also hosts festivals throughout the year, such as the Ueno Sakura Matsuri, or cherry blossom festival.

The Tokyo National Museum of Nature and Science is a popular museum located in Ueno

Park. It is home to over 20 million specimens, including dinosaur fossils and a planetarium. Visitors can explore the museum's many exhibits, as well as take part in interactive activities.

The Tokyo Tower is a communications tower in the city. The tower stands at 333 meters and is the second tallest structure in Japan. Visitors can take an elevator to the observation deck, where they can take in stunning views of Tokyo.

The Asakusa district is one of the oldest neighborhoods in Tokyo and is home to the famous Sensoji Temple. Visitors can explore the many shops and restaurants in the area, as well as take part in traditional festivals and ceremonies. There is also a shopping area called Nakamise-dori, where visitors can find souvenirs and traditional Japanese snacks.

Tokyo is an incredible city with so much to offer visitors. From temples and gardens to museums and theme parks, there is something for everyone in Tokyo. Whether you're looking for culture, history, or just a good time, Tokyo has something for you.

Popular Attractions in Osaka

Osaka is a vibrant city known for its nightlife, delicious food, and unique attractions. Whether you're a first-time visitor or a regular traveler, Osaka offers something for everyone. From historic temples and shrines to modern shopping malls and amusement parks, there's something to please everyone.

Here are 15 of the most popular attractions in Osaka that you should definitely visit during your stay.

Dotonbori – One of the most popular tourist districts in Osaka, Dotonbori is a bustling shopping, dining, and entertainment district located in the heart of the city. Shop for souvenirs, sample the city's famous street food, and admire the numerous neon signs that light up the area.

Don't forget to take a picture of the iconic Glico Man billboard.

Osaka Castle – Built in the 16th century, Osaka Castle is a symbol of the city's history. Visit the castle for a look at its beautiful grounds and grandiose architecture. The castle is surrounded by a moat and a number of stone walls and gates, making it an impressive sight to behold.

Shitennoji Temple – As one of the oldest temples in Japan, Shitennoji Temple has a long and important history. It is believed to have been founded by Prince Shotoku in the 6th century, and it still stands strong today. Visit the temple to learn about its fascinating history and enjoy its beautiful grounds.

Umeda Sky Building – The Umeda Sky Building is one of the tallest buildings in Osaka.

Take a trip to the top of the building for stunning views of the city and a chance to visit the rooftop observatory.

Universal Studios Japan – For a fun-filled day out, visit Universal Studios Japan. This movie-themed amusement park has a range of thrilling rides, shows, and attractions.

Amerikamura – Amerikamura, or "American Village," is a popular shopping district in Osaka. Visit for a chance to shop at trendy stores, sample delicious food, and experience Osaka's nightlife.

Tennoji Zoo – The Tennoji Zoo is one of the oldest zoos in Japan. Visit this attraction to view a variety of animals, from tigers and elephants to tropical birds.

Sumiyoshi Taisha – Sumiyoshi Taisha is an important Shinto shrine in Osaka. Visit the shrine to admire the traditional architecture and learn about the city's spiritual history.

Kuromon Ichiba Market – Visit Kuromon Ichiba Market to sample some of the freshest seafood in Japan. The market is a great place to try some of the city's famous sashimi and sushi.

Kaiyukan Aquarium – Kaiyukan Aquarium is one of the largest aquariums in the world. With a variety of fish, mammals, and reptiles, the aquarium is a great place to visit for a fun and educational day out.

Namba Parks – Namba Parks is an enormous mall located in the heart of Osaka. Visit the mall to shop for a variety of items, from clothes and electronics to souvenirs and snacks.

Tsutenkaku Tower – Tsutenkaku Tower offers stunning views of the city from its observation deck. Visit the tower for a chance to see the city from a different perspective.

Hozenji Yokocho – This narrow alley is located near Dotonbori and is filled with restaurants and shops. Visit Hozenji Yokocho to sample some of Osaka's best street food and browse the unique shops.

Spa World – Spa World is a luxurious spa located in the Tennoji district. Relax and unwind with a variety of treatments, from hot springs to massage.

Namba Grand Kagetsu Theater – Visit the Namba Grand Kagetsu Theater for a chance to experience traditional Japanese theater. The theater offers a variety of shows, from kabuki to comedy.

Popular Attractions in Kyoto

Kyoto is a city full of natural beauty and amazing cultural heritage, so it's no surprise that it's one of the most popular destinations for tourists in Japan. With its stunning temples and shrines, picturesque gardens, and delicious cuisine, Kyoto has something for everyone.

From the bustling streets of downtown Kyoto to the peaceful countryside, there are a variety of attractions that are sure to delight any visitor.

Here are 15 popular attractions in Kyoto that are sure to make your visit memorable.

Kinkaku-ji, or the Golden Pavilion, is one of Kyoto's most iconic landmarks. This stunning three-story pavilion is covered in gold leaf and is surrounded by a beautiful Japanese garden.

Visitors can take a tour of the grounds and explore the many halls and buildings. The top floor of the pavilion contains a Buddhist altar and a statue of the temple's founder, Ashikaga Yoshimitsu.

The Fushimi Inari Shrine is another popular attraction in Kyoto. This shrine is dedicated to the god of rice and sake, Inari. The shrine is composed of thousands of red torii gates that wind their way up the sacred mountain behind the shrine. Visitors can take a peaceful stroll through the gates and enjoy the peaceful atmosphere.

Kiyomizu-dera is a beautiful temple complex that was founded in the 8th century. It is one of the most popular temples in Japan and is home to a variety of cultural events and festivals. Visitors can explore the temple grounds and admire the remarkable architecture. The temple also has a number of restaurants, souvenir shops, and a lovely view of Kyoto from its wooden stage.

Gion is a popular geisha district in Kyoto. It is home to a variety of traditional teahouses and restaurants, as well as a number of geisha houses. Visitors can take a walk through the narrow streets and explore the many shops and restaurants. It's a great place to observe the traditional culture of Japan.

The Kyoto Imperial Palace is an important landmark in Kyoto. It was the residence of the Japanese emperor until 1868, and the palace grounds are open to the public. Visitors can explore the gardens and take in the stunning architecture.

Kyoto is home to a number of beautiful gardens. The most famous is the **Philosopher's Path**, a two-kilometer route along a canal lined with cherry trees. Visitors can stroll along the path and admire the cherry blossoms in the spring. The path is also home to a number of shrines and temples.

The Nijo Castle is a former imperial palace in Kyoto. The palace grounds are open to the public and visitors can explore the many halls and buildings. The castle also has a lovely garden and its walls are covered in beautiful paintings and carvings.

The Arashiyama Bamboo Grove is a stunning grove of bamboo trees located in the western part of Kyoto. Visitors can take a peaceful stroll through the grove and admire the tall bamboo stalks.

The Gion Matsuri is a traditional festival that takes place in Kyoto during the summer. The festival features a variety of traditional events such as parades, dances, and performances. Visitors can also enjoy traditional foods and drinks at the festival.

The Heian Shrine is a beautiful shrine that was built in 1895 to commemorate the 1100th anniversary of the founding of Kyoto. The shrine grounds are a popular spot for visitors and feature a number of gardens and ponds.

The Nishiki Market is a popular shopping district in Kyoto. The market is home to a variety of traditional stores and restaurants, as well as a number of souvenir shops. Visitors can grab a bite to eat and browse the many shops.

The Byodo-in Temple is a Buddhist temple located in the Uji area of Kyoto. The temple is home to a number of stunning statues and artwork, as well as a large pond filled with koi fish. Visitors can explore the grounds and admire the beautiful architecture.

Kurama-dera is a temple located in the hills north of Kyoto. The temple grounds are home to a number of shrines and temples, as well as a beautiful garden. Visitors can enjoy the peaceful atmosphere and take in the stunning views from the temple grounds.

The Tofuku-ji Temple is a Zen Buddhist temple located in the southern part of Kyoto. The temple grounds are home to a number of gardens and a popular teahouse. Visitors can take a tour of the grounds and explore the many halls and buildings.

The Nijo Castle Night Illumination is a popular event that takes place during the summer in Kyoto. The castle is illuminated with thousands of lights, creating a stunning display.

Visitors can take a stroll through the illuminated grounds and admire the beautiful night sky.

Outdoor Activities

Japan is a country full of outdoor activities to explore and enjoy. From its stunning mountain peaks to its beautiful beaches, there is something for everyone in the Land of the Rising Sun. From snow sports to beach activities, there's no shortage of fun and adventure to be had.

Here are just a few of the outdoor activities you can engage in while visiting Japan as a tourist.

1. Skiing and Snowboarding. Japan is home to some of the world's best ski resorts and snowboarding parks. With its powdery snow, steep slopes, and world-class ski resorts, Japan is a perfect destination for skiing and snowboarding. For those looking for a bit more adventure, there are also backcountry skiing and snowboarding options available.

2. Hiking. A great way to explore Japan's beautiful mountains is to go hiking. Japan has an impressive network of mountain trails and paths, ranging from easy walks to challenging multi-day treks. Whether you're looking for a leisurely stroll or a more strenuous trek, there's something for everyone in Japan's great mountain ranges.

3. Surfing. Japan is known for its excellent surfing spots. Whether you want to catch some waves in the Pacific Ocean or in one of Japan's many surf towns, you'll find plenty of opportunities for surfing. Many of Japan's beaches also offer excellent surfing conditions for all levels of surfers.

4. Kayaking. Kayaking is another great way to explore Japan's beautiful waterways. Whether you want to take a leisurely paddle down a river or challenge yourself with some white water rapids, there are plenty of options available. Kayaking is also a great way to see some of Japan's amazing wildlife, as many of the rivers and lakes are home to a variety of birds and animals.

5. Cycling. Japan is an incredibly bike-friendly country and has an extensive network of bike paths and trails. Whether you want to explore the countryside or take a leisurely ride around a city, there are plenty of options for cyclists. Many of Japan's cities also offer bike rentals, so you don't need to bring your own bike with you.

6. Swimming. Japan is a great place to go swimming, as it has some amazing beaches and hot springs. From crystal clear waters to thermal springs, there's something for everyone in Japan's beaches and hot springs.

7. Fishing. Fishing is one of the most popular outdoor activities in Japan. Whether you want to catch some fresh fish for dinner or just relax and enjoy the scenery, there are plenty of options for fishing in Japan. You can go on a day trip to one of Japan's many fishing spots or join a fishing tour for a more in-depth experience.

No matter what type of outdoor activity you're looking for, Japan has something for everyone. From skiing to surfing, kayaking to fishing, there's no shortage of amazing things to do while visiting Japan as a tourist.

So, what are you waiting for?

Get out and explore all that Japan has to offer.

Natural Wonders

Japan is home to some of the world's most stunning natural wonders. From majestic mountain ranges to tranquil lakes, Japan is a nature lover's paradise. From the northern island of Hokkaido to the southern island of Okinawa, Japan is filled with jaw-dropping natural beauty.

Here are 20 of Japan's most breathtaking natural wonders:

Mount Fuji: Japan's iconic and most recognizable landmark, Mount Fuji is the highest peak in the country at 3,776 meters. Located on the border of Shizuoka and Yamanashi Prefectures, Mt. Fuji is easily accessible by train and bus from Tokyo.

Aogashima Island: Aogashima is a volcanic island located in the Philippine Sea south of Tokyo. The island is home to a population of around 200 people and is surrounded by rugged cliffs and lush forests. Visitors can enjoy the stunning views from the top of the island's highest point, Mt. Io.

Shiretoko National Park: Located on the remote easternmost corner of Hokkaido, Shiretoko National Park is a UNESCO World Heritage Site.

This park is home to some of Japan's most pristine wilderness. The pristine forests, rugged coastline, and diverse wildlife make this one of Japan's most beautiful national parks.

Hakone: Located in Kanagawa Prefecture, Hakone is a popular hot-spring resort area and is home to stunning views of Mt. Fuji. The area is known for its many hot-spring resorts and Onsen, and the picturesque Lake Ashi.

Akan National Park: Akan National Park is located in the northernmost part of Hokkaido and is home to some of Japan's most stunning natural scenery. The park features pristine alpine forests, stunning lakes, and hot-spring resorts.

Kamikochi: Kamikochi is a beautiful alpine valley located in the Japanese Alps of Nagano Prefecture. The area is home to lush forests, crystal-clear rivers, and stunning mountain views.

Kegon Falls: Kegon Falls is a stunning 97-meter tall waterfall located in Nikko National Park. The falls are accessible by a ropeway and the observation deck provides stunning views of the surrounding area.

Kurikoma Volcano: Kurikoma Volcano is an active stratovolcano located in Miyagi Prefecture. The volcano is surrounded by lush forests and is home to many hot-spring resorts.

Takachiho Gorge: Takachiho Gorge is a stunning canyon located in Miyazaki Prefecture. The gorge is home to many waterfalls, caves and hot-spring resorts.

Shiraito Falls: Shiraito Falls is a stunning waterfall located in the Fujinomiya area of Shizuoka Prefecture. The waterfall is fed by underground springs and cascades down a steep cliff face.

Amanohashidate: Amanohashidate is a stunning natural sandbar located in Kyoto Prefecture. The area is home to pine trees, beautiful beaches and stunning views of the sandbar from the mountain.

Kumano Kodo: Kumano Kodo is a network of ancient pilgrimage routes located in the Kii Peninsula of Wakayama Prefecture. The area is home to stunning forests, shrines and hot-spring resorts.

Koyasan: Koyasan is a UNESCO World Heritage Site located in Wakayama Prefecture. The area is home to stunning temples, forests and hot-spring resorts.

Kushiro Marsh: Kushiro Marsh is the largest marsh in Japan and is located in Hokkaido. The area is home to a diverse range of wildlife and is a popular spot for bird-watching.

Kirishima Mountains: The Kirishima Mountains are located in Kagoshima Prefecture and are home to stunning views, hot-spring resorts, and hiking trails.

Mount Kaimon: Mount Kaimon is an active volcano located in Kagoshima Prefecture. The volcano is home to lush forests and stunning views of the surrounding area.

Okinawa Churaumi Aquarium: The Okinawa Churaumi Aquarium is the world's largest aquarium and is located in Okinawa Prefecture. The aquarium is home to a diverse range of marine life, including whale sharks and manta rays.

Lake Toya: Lake Toya is a stunning lake located in Hokkaido. The lake is home to pristine forests, hot-spring resorts, and stunning views.

Hachimantai National Park: Hachimantai National Park is located in Iwate Prefecture and is home to stunning forests, lakes, and hot-spring resorts.

Mount Zao: Mount Zao is an active volcano located in Yamagata Prefecture. The volcano is home to stunning views, hot-spring resorts, and hiking trails.

Lake Biwa: Lake Biwa is the largest lake in Japan and is located in Shiga Prefecture. The lake is home to stunning views and is a popular spot for fishing and boating.

No matter which natural wonder you choose to explore, you're sure to be captivated by the beauty and tranquility of Japan's nature. To get to most of these natural wonders, you can take a train or bus from Tokyo. Alternatively, you can rent a car and take a self-drive tour.

Festivals

When it comes to Japanese festivals, there is so much to explore and experience. Whether you're a lifelong resident of Japan or a tourist visiting the country for the first time, you'll find that there are many incredible festivals to attend.

From traditional rituals to modern celebrations, the festivals of Japan capture the culture, history, and spirit of the Land of the Rising Sun.

Here is a list of some of the most popular and unique Japanese festivals that a tourist should know about:

1. **Setsubun** – Setsubun is one of the most famous Japanese festivals and is held annually on February 3rd. It celebrates the arrival of spring and the end of winter. During the festival,

people traditionally wear a demon mask and throw roasted beans at the mask to drive away evil spirits.

2. Hina Matsuri – Hina Matsuri is held annually on March 3rd and is a festival that honors girls. During the festival, dolls in the shapes of the Imperial Court are displayed in homes and small shrines are set up in front of houses.

3. Hanami – Hanami is a popular festival in Japan celebrated in the spring. It's a time to enjoy the beauty of nature and appreciate the flowering of cherry blossoms. People typically gather in parks or along rivers to enjoy the view and have picnics.

4. Tanabata – Tanabata is held annually on July 7th and is a festival that celebrates the stars Vega and Altair. During the festival people write wishes on strips of paper and hang them on bamboo branches.

5. Obon – Obon is an annual festival that honors the spirits of ancestors. It's usually held in August and is a time for people to remember their loved ones and celebrate their lives.

6. Awa Odori – Awa Odori is held annually in August in Tokushima Prefecture. It's one of the most famous festivals in Japan and features traditional music and dancing.

7. Jidai Matsuri – Jidai Matsuri is held annually on October 22nd in Kyoto. It's a festival that celebrates the history of Japan and features a procession of people in costumes from different eras of Japanese history.

8. Shichi-go-san – Shichi-go-san is held annually on November 15th and is a festival that celebrates the growth and health of children aged three, five, and seven. During the festival, parents take their children to shrines where the children are blessed with good fortune.

9. New Year's – New Year's is one of the most important holidays in Japan and is celebrated on January 1st. It's a time to celebrate the new year, reflect on the past, and make resolutions for the future.

If you're looking for a unique and exciting way to experience the culture of Japan, attending one of these festivals is a great way to do it.

From traditional rituals to modern celebrations, the festivals of Japan capture the culture, history, and spirit of the Land of the Rising Sun.

Shopping

When it comes to shopping in Japan, there is a wide array of options available to tourists. From traditional markets and department stores to modern shopping malls and specialty stores, Japan offers something for everyone. Whether you're looking for traditional goods, the latest fashion trends, or souvenirs to take home, Japan has it all.

For a traditional shopping experience, nothing beats the hustle and bustle of Japan's markets and department stores. The Tsukiji fish market in Tokyo is one of the most famous markets in the world, where you can buy fresh seafood and watch the tuna auctions.

The Ameya Yokocho in Tokyo is a great place to find cheap souvenirs, from traditional snacks to questionable trinkets. Other traditional markets include the Asakusa Kannon Temple shopping street and the Nakamise Shopping Street.

When it comes to department stores, Japan has some of the biggest and best in the world. These department stores are great for finding high-end brands and luxury items.

The Takashimaya Department Store in Tokyo is one of the most famous, with its huge selection of fashion, home goods and more. The Mitsukoshi Department Store in Tokyo is another great option, as it offers both luxury brands and traditional Japanese items.

For a modern shopping experience, Japan is home to some of the world's most impressive shopping malls. The Tokyo Midtown in Roppongi is a great place to shop for designer labels, as well as enjoy a range of entertainment and dining options.

The Shibuya 109 department store, located in the heart of Tokyo's hip shopping district, is a great place to find the latest fashion trends. The Shibuya Hikarie, also located in Shibuya, is a great shopping and entertainment complex with a wide range of stores and restaurants.

For those looking for unique and specialty items, Japan is home to a range of specialty shops. The Yaesu Shopping Arcade in Tokyo is a great place to find traditional Japanese items, such as kimonos, yukatas and fans.

The Akihabara Electric Town is the place to go for all your electronics needs, with a vast array of stores selling everything from video games to cameras. The Kappabashi Kitchen Town is a great place to find all kinds of kitchenware and tableware, from traditional Japanese items to modern kitchen gadgets.

Finally, no trip to Japan is complete without visiting one of its many souvenir shops. These shops have a range of traditional and modern items, from traditional snacks and souvenirs to modern electronics.

The Nipponbashi Denden Town in Osaka is a great place to find all kinds of gadgets, from retro video games to modern electronics. The Ginza Shopping District in Tokyo is a great place for luxury items, as well as souvenirs.

Whether you're looking for traditional goods, the latest fashion trends, or souvenirs to take home, Japan has something for everyone. From traditional markets and department stores to modern shopping malls and specialty stores, Japan offers an unparalleled shopping experience.

Nightlife

When it comes to nightlife in Japan as a tourist, there is a lot to explore. Japan is a country with a long, rich history and its culture is one that is steeped in tradition and holds a strong importance for the present and future generations.

Japan is also a country that is renowned for its vibrant nightlife and its many attractions. In the larger cities like Tokyo and Osaka, you can find a wide variety of places to explore and experience.

One of the most popular places to visit in Japan at night is the famous Kabukicho district in Tokyo. This area is home to a variety of bars, nightclubs, and restaurants. The atmosphere here is lively and relaxed and is a great place to meet people and mingle. Whether you're looking for a casual night out or a wild night of partying, you can find something to do in Kabukicho.

Another popular nightlife spot in Japan is Shinjuku. This area of Tokyo is known for its many clubs, bars, and restaurants, as well as its lively atmosphere.

There are many places to explore here, whether you're looking for a quiet dinner or a wild night out.

If you're looking for more of a cultural experience, then don't miss out on the opportunity to visit a traditional Japanese Izakaya bar. These bars are known for their warm and friendly atmosphere, and they offer a variety of food and drinks that are sure to satisfy.

It's a great way to get a taste of Japan's culture and learn more about its traditional customs.

Finally, if you're looking for a more luxurious experience, then there are many high-end clubs and bars in Japan that offer a more upscale experience. These clubs are perfect for those looking for an evening of fine dining and dancing.

No matter what type of nightlife experience you're looking for in Japan, there's sure to be something that suits your taste. Whether you're looking for a wild night out or a more relaxed evening, Japan has something to offer everyone.

So what are you waiting for?

Get out there and explore the nightlife in Japan.

Popular Souvenirs

As a tourist to Japan, you'll likely want to bring home a souvenir that captures the spirit of your trip and the unique culture of this fascinating country. But with so many options to choose from, it can be hard to decide which souvenirs to buy.

One of the most popular souvenirs for tourists in Japan are the unique regional specialty items. From the delicate paper umbrellas of Kyoto to the intricately designed Kanazawa gold leaf, each prefecture has its own one-of-a-kind souvenirs that make great gifts and will remind you of your time in Japan.

Another popular item to buy as a souvenir is kimono fabric, which is available in many different colors and patterns, and is often used to make bags, purses, wallets, and other items. It's a great way to bring a piece of Japan home with you.

Sake and tea are another popular souvenir, as these are two of Japan's most popular beverages. Sake is often sold in traditional Japanese bottles and can be a great gift for someone special. Tea, on the other hand, is usually sold in tins or bags, and there are many varieties to choose from.

For those looking for something a bit more unique, there are also a wide range of traditional Japanese crafts available as souvenirs. These include items such as pottery, lacquerware, and even wooden dolls.

These items are often handcrafted and can be a great way to bring home a piece of Japanese culture.

Finally, food items make great souvenirs as well. From tasty snacks like mochi and senbei to traditional Japanese sweets like manju and dango, there are plenty of food items to choose from.

And if you're looking for a more substantial gift, you can even find traditional Japanese food items such as sushi and soba noodles.

No matter what souvenirs you choose, they will be a lasting reminder of your trip to Japan and the amazing culture of this country. So don't forget to pick up some souvenirs during your travels in Japan.

Chapter 6

Health & Safety

Safety & Security

Safety and security is an important factor to consider when traveling to Japan. As a foreign tourist, you may be unfamiliar with the culture, laws, and customs of the country. It is important to take extra precautions to ensure your safety.

In general, Japan is a safe country and crime rates are very low. However, there are certain situations and areas that you should be aware of and take extra precautions.

First, it is important to be aware of your surroundings. Be aware of possible pickpockets and scam artists. Be sure to keep your valuables out of sight and in a secure location. Avoid walking alone late at night and in secluded areas. While public transportation is generally safe, it is important to be aware of your surroundings and keep your personal items close.

Second, it is important to be aware of the cultural differences between Japan and your home country. Respect the customs and culture of the country and be aware of local laws. It is important to be aware of the language barrier and be aware that English may not be widely spoken in certain areas.

Third, it is important to know your rights as a tourist in Japan. While the Japanese court system is similar to that of the United States, there are differences. Be sure to familiarize yourself with the laws and regulations in Japan.

Finally, it is important to be aware of the natural disasters that can occur in Japan. Earthquakes, tsunamis, and typhoons are all possible. Be sure to stay informed about the weather and possible disasters that can occur.

These are just a few safety tips for tourists in Japan. It is important to be aware of your surroundings, be respectful of the culture and customs, and stay informed about the weather and possible disasters.

General Safety Tips for Tourists in Japan:

• Be aware of your surroundings and keep your valuables out of sight.

• Respect the culture and customs of Japan.

• Be aware of the language barrier and know that English may not be widely spoken.

• Be aware of your rights as a tourist and familiarize yourself with the laws and regulations.

• Stay informed about the weather and possible disasters.

• Avoid walking alone late at night and in secluded areas.

• Use public transportation, but be aware of your surroundings and keep your personal items close.

Laws & Regulations

If you're planning on traveling to Japan, it's important to know the laws and regulations for tourists in the country. There are many things to take into consideration, from cultural norms to safety precautions.

Here is all there is to know about laws and regulations for tourists in Japan.

Customs:

When entering Japan, you must declare any items that you may be bringing in with you, such as food and souvenirs. You must also declare any items that may be subject to restrictions or special rules, such as firearms, drugs, and pornographic materials. Additionally, Japan has strict regulations on importing and exporting foreign currency.

Visas:

Most tourists to Japan are required to obtain a visa prior to entering the country. Depending on your nationality and the purposes of your visit, you may need to obtain a specific type of visa. It is important to check the requirements for your specific visa before arriving in Japan.

Safety:

Japan is generally a very safe country, but it's important to take certain precautions to ensure your safety. It is important to be aware of your surroundings and to avoid dangerous areas.

Additionally, it is recommended to stay in well-lit areas at night, and to avoid walking alone in unfamiliar areas. It is also important to lock your doors and windows when leaving your accommodation.

Transportation:

Public transportation in Japan is efficient and reliable, and is the most common form of transportation for tourists. When using public transportation, it is important to be aware of the rules and regulations.

For example, eating and drinking on public transportation is prohibited, and it is important to be respectful of other passengers. Additionally, it is important to ensure that you have the correct fare and tickets for your journey.

Culture:

Japan is steeped in culture, and it is important to be aware of the customs and traditions of the country. It is important to be respectful of cultural norms, such as bowing when greeting someone, and to avoid inappropriate behavior, such as public displays of affection. Additionally, it is important to be aware of the dress code, and to avoid wearing clothing that is too revealing.

Additional Safety Tips:

1. Always be aware of your surroundings and avoid dangerous areas.

2. Stay in well-lit areas at night, and avoid walking alone in unfamiliar areas.

3. Lock your doors and windows when leaving your accommodation.

4. Be respectful of cultural norms and traditions.

5. Dress appropriately, and avoid wearing clothing that is too revealing.

6. Follow the rules and regulations when using public transportation.

7. Be aware of the requirements for entering and leaving the country.

8. Declare any items that may be subject to restrictions or special rules.

9. Familiarize yourself with the laws and regulations for tourists in Japan.

10. Practice general safety precautions and use common sense.

Medical Services & Emergency Contact Information

Travelling to Japan is an exciting experience full of unique culture, sights, and experiences. Many tourists come to Japan to enjoy the beautiful scenery and delicious food. However, if you become ill during your stay, it is important to be aware of the medical services available in Japan.

For visitors to Japan, medical services are available both in hospitals and clinics. Depending on your condition, you may need to visit both types of facilities. Hospitals in Japan are staffed by highly trained physicians and nurses and provide comprehensive medical services, including specialized care for serious illnesses and injuries.

Clinics are usually less expensive than hospitals and are usually staffed by general practitioners and nurses. Clinics specialize in treating minor illnesses and injuries.

When visiting a hospital or clinic in Japan, you will need to bring your passport and a copy of your insurance policy. Most hospitals and clinics in Japan accept credit cards, but it is best to check with the facility in advance. If you do not have health insurance coverage, you will have to pay for any medical services you receive.

If you need to see a doctor or require medical treatment, you should make an appointment at a hospital or clinic near your location. It is also possible to make an appointment online or by phone.

When you arrive at the hospital or clinic, you will need to sign in and fill out a form with your personal information. You should also bring a copy of your passport and a valid health insurance policy.

If you need to be admitted to a hospital for treatment, you will be required to fill out a form with your medical history and provide a sample of your blood and urine. Depending on your condition, you may also be required to undergo medical tests such as X-rays or CT scans.

In addition to hospitals and clinics, there are also pharmacies in Japan where you can purchase over-the-counter medications. Pharmacists in Japan are usually very knowledgeable about medications and can provide you with advice about the best treatment for your condition.

It is important to note that many medications available in Japan may not be available in other countries.

Japan also has a number of emergency services available for visitors. If you have a medical emergency, you can call **119** for an ambulance or you can go to the nearest hospital.

Emergency services are available 24 hours a day, seven days a week and are free of charge.

Medical services in Japan are generally of a high quality and accessible to all visitors. While it is important to be aware of the medical services available, it is also important to remember to practice good health habits to reduce the risk of getting sick.

Make sure to drink plenty of fluids, get enough rest and exercise, and follow the recommended vaccinations for your trip. By taking these precautions, you will be able to enjoy your stay in Japan without any worries.

Chapter 7

Tips for successful Travel

Money

When you're visiting Japan as a tourist, you may be wondering about the local currency and how you'll go about obtaining it. Knowing the basics of Japanese money can help make your visit a bit easier and less stressful.

The currency of Japan is the Japanese Yen. It is denoted by the symbol ¥ and is subdivided into 100 sen. Currently, the exchange rate is around 1 U.S. dollar to 108 Japanese Yen. Japanese Yen is available in coins and notes of various denominations. The coins are available in 1, 5, 10, 50, 100 and 500 Yen denominations. The notes come in 1,000, 2,000, 5,000 and 10,000 Yen denominations.

One of the best places to exchange money in Japan is at the airport. Most of the major international airports in Japan have currency exchange counters where you can exchange your foreign currency into Japanese Yen. There are also many banks and post offices throughout the country that offer currency exchange services. You can also use ATMs in Japan to withdraw cash in Japanese Yen.

When it comes to credit cards and debit cards, Japan is a bit different than other countries. Most establishments in Japan accept credit cards and debit cards issued by banks outside of Japan, but you may have difficulty using them at smaller businesses. Be sure to check with the business before attempting to pay with a foreign credit or debit card.

Traveller's checks are also accepted in Japan, but they are not as widely accepted as in other countries. It is best to exchange your traveller's checks for Japanese Yen at a bank or post office before attempting to use them.

Finally, you may want to consider bringing a small amount of Japanese Yen with you when you visit Japan. This way, you won't have to worry about exchanging money right away or having to look for an ATM.

Knowing the basics of Japanese money can help make your visit to Japan a bit easier and less stressful. Be sure to exchange your foreign currency into Japanese Yen before your trip and to bring a small amount of Japanese Yen with you just in case.

You may also want to familiarize yourself with the different denominations of coins and notes so that you can easily recognize them while you're in Japan.

Japanese Basics To Know

As a tourist visiting Japan, learning some basic Japanese language is sure to make your visit more enjoyable. Not only will it help you communicate with locals, but it will also demonstrate your respect for the culture and tradition of Japan.

To get started, let's look at some of the most important Japanese words to know.

First, let's look at Japanese greetings. Saying "Konnichiwa" (Hello) is a great way to start a conversation. Similarly, "Ohayo gozaimasu" (Good morning), "Konbanwa" (Good evening), and "Sayonara" (Goodbye) are all good phrases to know.

Next, let's look at basic phrases for ordering food. Knowing how to say "Kore wo kudasai" (I'll have this) and "Sumimasen" (Excuse me) will come in very handy.

When shopping, you will want to know how to say "Ikura desu ka?" (How much is this?) and "Arigatou gozaimasu" (Thank you).

It is also useful to know how to ask for directions. Knowing "Dochira desu ka?" (Where is it?) and "Migigawa desu ka?" (Is it to the right?) will come in very handy.

Finally, it is important to learn some basic numbers. Knowing how to count from 1 to 10 (ichi, ni, san, shi, go, roku, shichi, hachi, ku, juu) will be very useful when asking for directions, ordering food, and shopping.

These are just some of the basics of the Japanese language, but they are sure to come in handy during your stay in Japan. With a little practice, you will be able to get around much more easily, and you will be able to appreciate the wonderful culture of Japan even more.

Conclusion

If you've been lucky enough to travel to Japan, you know that the country is truly a unique, awe-inspiring place. From its stunning landscapes, to its fascinating culture and traditions, to its delicious cuisine, Japan has something to offer everyone.

Whether you're looking to explore the country's beautiful nature, experience the hustle and bustle of its cities, or simply relax and enjoy the peacefulness of its rural areas, Japan has something for everyone.

No matter how long your Japan trip is, there is no shortage of things to do and see. The country is full of beautiful temples, ancient castles, and stunning gardens. The food is incredible, the people are warm and friendly, and the culture is unlike anything else in the world. Whether you're traveling alone, with family, or with friends, Japan is sure to be an unforgettable experience.

So, if you're looking for an unforgettable destination to explore, Japan is the perfect place. With its unique culture, gorgeous nature, and friendly people, Japan is sure to be an unforgettable experience.

Whether you're looking to explore the bustling cities, relax in the quiet countryside, or simply enjoy some of the delicious food, Japan has something for everyone.

So, pack your bags and get ready to explore one of the most beautiful countries in the world.

Printed in Great Britain
by Amazon

19603312R00112